BUTTERFLY BLOODLINE

POEMS FROM A SOUL
TRANSFORMED BY THE CROSS

By Niki Hutchins

Copyright Page

Table of Contents

Dedication

I want to honor my Lord and Savior, Jesus Christ, because if it weren't for Him, I wouldn't be alive to share this story or bring hope to others. Jesus is, and will always be my best friend. I also want to honor my late husband, who was my closest friend on this earth—your memory lives on, and I thank you for your prayers. To my parents, my children, my sisters and brothers by blood, and those in the body of Christ, as well as to everyone who has spoken a kind word or offered encouragement along the way—you all mean the world to me, and I love you.

Introduction

I once believed my story was too broken to ever be put back together. Addiction sank its claws into me, shame pressed down like a weight I couldn't shake, and I thought I had burned every bridge worth crossing. Maybe you've felt that way too — trapped in a cycle that feels unbreakable, drowning in choices you can't undo, wondering if freedom could ever be real.

But here's the truth I discovered: no matter how far you've gone, you are never too far from grace. I should not be standing here, writing these words. Yet the same God who spoke light into the darkness spoke life into me when I was sure I had none left. He stepped into my chaos, lifted me from the pit, and showed me that His mercy runs deeper than my mistakes.

This book is not just poetry — it's testimony. It carries fire from the nights I thought I wouldn't survive, and it carries hope from the mornings when joy broke through like sunlight. It is proof that Jesus leaves the ninety-nine to chase down the one — and I was that one. If He came for me, He will come for you too.

Addiction tried to silence me. Shame tried to bury me. But grace had the final word. And the same grace that raised me can raise you.

Butterfly Bloodline was birthed from pain, but it breathes victory. These pages are soaked in struggle, but they shine with redemption. If you've ever felt trapped, if you've ever been lost, if you've ever thought your life was beyond repair — hear me now: it's not over. Freedom in Christ is real, and it's closer than you think.

This book is called Butterfly Bloodline because my life is living proof of transformation. I was cocooned in darkness, but He broke me into light. I was chained to addiction, but now I am covered by the blood of Jesus. My old bloodline carried pain and shame, but now I carry His. And these poems? They are the wings He gave me to rise above it all.

So turn the page. Open your heart. Let these words remind you that chains can break, hearts can heal, and lives can rise again.

Welcome to Butterfly Bloodline.

Let's fly.

"But those who hope in the Lord will renew
their strength.
They will soar on wings like eagles;
they will run and not grow weary,
they will walk and not be faint"

Isaiah 40:31

SECTION ONE:

WINGS (Rising in Grace)

BIG-TIME DREAM

Just a small-town girl
With a big-time dream,

Surrounded by obstacles,
I take in the scene.

Learning to watch and pray,
I move with strategy—
Taming every feeling
That could lead to tragedy.

By keeping my composure,
I rise above the odds.
I'm devoted to the Master;
I serve no other gods.

Thrown into the fire,
I'm tested in the flames.
Unmoved by ambition,
untouched by the games."

But the fire wasn't pretty—
It nearly took me out.
The enemy hated my purpose,
So he filled me with doubt.

He wanted me dead,
Wanted me silent and numb—
But God had a plan,
So I learned to overcome.

Now this is my chance—
I'm living the dream.
Once lost in addiction,
Now I'm sober and clean.

All my life,
I was scared to go all in…
But here I stand,
Wearing a big grin.

And this dream?
It's more than a stage or rhyme—
It's to tell the world about Jesus,
One poem at a time.

Surrounded by obstacles,
I take in the scene—
Just a small-town girl
With a big-time dream.

MERCY'S KISS

Mercy's kiss—
the sweetest I've ever known.
If you had seen me back then,
you would know how much I've grown.

The struggles meant to break me
were used by God to shape me.

I stared at death for too long,
until I chose truth
and found where I belong.

They said I'd never amount to anything,
they tried to silence my voice.
Their sharp words cut deep;
they left me with no choice.

Lies kept me bound up tight
Leaving me restless through the night.
I forgot how to laugh
and felt the weight of the aftermath.

I turned into a victim,
but not anymore.
Sticks and stones can't shake me
like they did before.

Now I know what I once missed:
there's nothing sweeter
than mercy's kiss.

It's the healing touch—
the kind that restores.
It pulled me from chaos
and opened new doors.

The sweetest love
I've ever known.
If you had seen me back then,
you would see how much I've grown.

And now I rise with this truth:
I can't miss—
there's nothing sweeter
than mercy's kiss

GROWING PAINS

Growing pains may sting,
yet they make us strong.
Without the struggle,
there would be no song.

Hearts grow heavy,
and teardrops fall—
but in those moments,
we learn who we can call.

Some days feel too heavy to bear—
thank God for those
who simply care.

Hard times reveal what I couldn't see:
not just my strength,
but Christ alive in me.

Love conquers the fears
I once tried to hide.
It reaches deep
and heals from the inside.

When the road ahead feels unclear,
God whispers to my spirit:
"I am right here."

Without the fire,
we'd never be refined.
So I release the weight
and let His will align.

Wings mended in the furnace,
feathers catch the light.
It's time to fly—
and it's alright.

Now I'm grateful
for what remains:
Jesus in me,
flowing through my veins—

Giving purpose,
breathing life again,
washing me clean,
my Savior, my Friend.

So let the fire
reshape my frame;
I live to honor
Jesus' name.

What once was loss
is now my gain—
His glory shines
through growing pains.

THE STILL SMALL VOICE

Here I am at Your feet again.
The voices are loud,
but You're not in the wind.

You're the still, small voice—
a gentle whisper in my ear.
And just like David before Goliath,
I will not fear.

Foxes creep in,
so I watch where I step.
They're hiding everywhere,
waiting to snare what's left.

Wide awake—
I can't afford to sleep.
The waves rise high,
but You pull me from the deep.

Darkness can't hold me;
light breaks the night.
This battle isn't mine—
the war belongs to Christ.

The still, small voice
speaks like a river that flows.
If I'm putting trust in anyone,
it's the One who knows.

I try my best—
but for some, it's never enough.
Yet that's not important;
Your truth is what I trust.

Even with miracles,
people still beg for proof.
But I've tasted Your goodness—
and I'm living the truth.

These are the days
when sorrow runs deep,
but You teach me to turn
from anger I'd keep.

Though none go with me,
still I will go.
You turn up the heat,
but You help me grow.

Some days I feel the target,
as the arrows attack—
but it's Your oil on me,
And I know that for a fact.

Here I am at Your feet again.
The voices are loud,
but You're not in the wind.

You're the still, small voice—
a gentle whisper in my ear.
And just like David before Goliath,
I will not fear.

THE BETHEL GIRL

Here's a cool story—
Let me explain…
Bethel Colony of Mercy helped me process
heartache and pain.

I met sisters and brothers,
friends I'll never forget—
'Cause Bethel folks?
They don't let you quit.

Forever family—
yeah, we're tight.
Praise the Lord,
we light up the night.

This place taught me
discipline and love,
but most of all—
about the goodness of God above.

And no matter how hard
I tried not to stay,
that Bethel love
never turned me away.

So come prepared
to give your three thankfuls,
and make real friends
whose love never cancels.

I love that mountain—
it gives my soul peace.
A refuge,
where God brought me release.

The staff is kind,
good people—rare to find.
If you're in addiction
or ready to be free,
give Bethel a whirl…

come see what I see.

At Bethel I found
the courage to sing,
Mercy and love
gave me back my wings.

Sincerely,
with love,
The Bethel Girl

TO THE ONES WHO PAVED THE WAY

To the saints who paved the way
With prayers that touched God's ears,
To the ones who held on in faith
Through trials, storms, and tears—

To the leaders who love
And live just to serve,
To the brothers in Christ
And the mothers with nerve—

To the ones who clean the church,
Who cook with love and grace,
To the ones who preach that Word
And speak truth face to face.

To those who paved the way
At a holy, heavy cost—
Not just loving some,
But loving all that's lost.

To the ones who never give up,
Who always stand and fight,
To the brothers and sisters
Who are friends through darkest nights—

To the ones who don't even see
How their stories changed us for the good,
To the weary and the worn-out,
Who feel misunderstood.

To the ones who may never know
How special they truly are…
It's because of the ones who paved the way
That we've made it this far.

To the ones in the background
Who never feel seen—
Thank you for showing up
And making us feel like a team.

To the ones who wonder
If their cries have gone unheard—
Just look at me.
Someone prayed,
And God honored every word.

So I just wanna say thank you
For all that you do…
You are saints,
And we truly love you.

THE LINE IN THE SAND

I am the line in the sand.
Throwing stones at me won't help—
I hope you understand.

I'm brave enough to try.
Even with one wing,
I still lift others,
hoping they will fly.

People will talk; they always do.
But I place it in God's hands
and let Him carry me through.

I'm not perfect,
and I won't pretend.
I stumble, I rise,
but His grace never ends.

What am I worth?
A love that never makes me guess,
a love that covers me in every mess.

A love that stays when times get rough,
a love that whispers, "You are enough."

So rare. So true.
A love that only comes from You.

I live for the Lord—
not flawless, but held by His hand.
When I'm weak, He lifts me.
By His strength, I stand.

There's only one me,
and I refuse to drown.
When the waves crash hard,
His mercy pulls me around.

I talk to everyone—
that's just who I am.
And I pray to the Father
that each soul finds the Lamb.

Some people love it.
Some people don't.
If you ask me to change,
I'll smile—but I won't.

If I say I've got you,
then trust that I do.
But even at my best,
I might still fail you too.

No need to pretend—
sometimes, I bend.
But the line in the sand?
That's Jesus, my Friend.

DANCE LIKE DAVID

So what if I dance like David?
It's my soul that shines through.
I'll spin in the streets like I'm crazy,
'Cause His joy makes me new.

There's no fire without a spark;
Faith alone
Was enough for Noah to build the ark.

People curse and fuss,
Making their scene—
But all I want
Is to serve my King.

They say I fit in,
But I know I don't.
I was made to stand out,
And change? I won't.

For those in the back,
Let me say it again:
I was never created
To blend in with them.

I love everyone,
But it's plain to see
Not all love me back—
Some talk secretly.

And that's fine—
I've walked that road before.
But not anymore…
Now sticks and stones just make me roar.

Growing pains push me higher—
God lives in me,
So I burn with His fire.

I need the rain—
Though I cry at times,
There's always purpose
In the climb.
And when it fades,
I'll face the next test.
I may not like it…
But I know God knows best.

To whom much is given,
Much is required;
And a heart like Jesus—
That's what I desire.

Lord, I am Yours,
Though the trials are many;
Still I'll stand ready,
'Cause You've given me plenty.

So I'll keep my eyes sharp,
Never leaving my post.
Even if I stumble,
I'll lean on the Holy Ghost.

Keep me alert,
Let my spirit discern.
There's a fire in me—
So let it burn.

And when the battle is over,
The enemy's plans frustrated,
You'll still find me in the streets—
Dancing like David.

WILD AND FREE

Wild and free—
yeah, that's me.
Marching to the beat
of my own drum.
His name is Jesus,
and He has overcome.

Every obstacle
that blocks my path,
I'll walk right through—
God does the math.

No longer in chains,
no weights pulling me down.
I'm counting up the jewels
He's placing in my crown.

It's nothing I've done;
I could never earn this love.
So I lay it all down
for the One above.

And the One above?
He reaches for the rest.
There's power in that—
I had to confess.

Wild and free—
yeah, that's me.
Still dancing like David,
for the world to see.

So lace 'em up,
let's run this race.
Hungry for the Word,
I'm fueled by grace.

It's not religion—
it's relationship true.
I've made my decision:
I'm following You.

I'm gonna love hard,
no matter what's done.
You can't see a hater
when you're focused on the Son.

Can't tame me—
I was born to be.
If you knew what I knew,
you'd shout it with me:

Wild and free—
yeah, that's still me.

THE JESUS IN ME

Call it what you want—
it don't matter to me.
I've got one mission:
Kingdom victory.

Beyond the stage,
there's smoke that blows…
But I don't chase winds—
I serve the One who knows.

Even the angels
bow at His throne.
If you don't love Him,
you'll stand alone.

I wasn't always bold—
I used to hide my flame.
But Jesus lit a fire,
and I ain't never been the same.

Maybe it's a stranger,
or a kid on the block—
one look at you
could make them stop.

To some of them,
we're the only light they'll see.
That's why I pray
they see the Jesus in me.

So let my walk be real,
my words stay true.
If they see Jesus—
let them see Him through and through.

And when my race is done,
may this be my decree:
I lived my life
so they'd see the Jesus in me.

WE WALK IN THE LIGHT

It's such a blessing—
sometimes I hold back tears in the testing.
Other times, I let them fall…
but I count on God through it all.

He told me the truth from the start:
"Baby girl, guard your heart."

The struggle is real—
but so is He.
One whisper of His name,
and demons flee.

Blessings show up as peace and joy,
not just in things you can buy or enjoy.
You'll see it one day—just wait, my friend.
God's timing is perfect from start to end.

Anointed now,
appointed later—
I stand in faith,
leaning on my Creator.

I'm giving my all,
refusing to fall.
I might look small,
but in Him, I'm tall.

And if they never clap?
That's more than okay.
Less of me,
and more of Him every day.

Clout doesn't move me—
truth does.
I walk with purpose,
simply because…

We walk in light,
because His blood made us new.
Butterfly bloodline—
breaking through.

Wings once broken
now carry me high…
proof that the caterpillar
was always meant to fly.

PEACE, BE STILL

Speak to the storm
until the winds obey.
There is power
in the words we say.

It's not about what we think—
it's about what we know.
The harvest will always
reflect what we sow.

Less of me,
more of You.
How can something false
ever be true?

Returning to my first love,
never looking back.
Foxes have holes—
and they're quick to attack.

I'm gentle now,
can't afford to lose my cool again.
Some smile in your face…
but that don't make them friends.

Their opinions never
got me far.
People talk all the time—
but that doesn't say who they are.

If you knew where I've been,
you'd understand my stride.
The same Man who saved me
was the One I denied.

They say, "Watch who you love—
you're too nice, girl, be smart."
I'm not slow—
I just got a lot of heart.

I remember where
God brought me from.
Just because I'm kind
doesn't mean I'm dumb.

If loving people is wrong,
then I'll take the blame.
I've been loving people—
I'll keep doing the same.

Burning coals on the enemy's head—
that's what it means
to be Spirit-led.

Peace, be still—
that's all I can say.
The storm may rage,
but God has His way.

And when the winds rise,
I stand unshaken still—
For Christ is the Word,
and His voice says:
"Peace, be still."

LOVE LETTERS TO JESUS

My soul belongs,
my heart bursts out in songs—
hymns of freedom rise,
like psalms that touch the skies.

I've written love letters, a million or more,
to Jesus, the One my soul adores.
I need Him deeper than breath, than life,
my refuge, my peace in struggle and strife.

I try to be still, but the flames won't die;
there's a holy fire burning inside.

Life takes its toll,
a tug-of-war for my soul.
The battle in my mind rages on,
where weapons are heavy

and nights feel long.

Still, I strive to balance
these God-given talents.

Wearing a coat of many colors—
a gift I could never earn alone.
Through all my failures,
His mercy made it known.

Religious spirits try to silence my voice,
to chain my words,
as if I had no choice.

I've taken many blows,
and only God knows
the scars carved deep in my heart.
But He heals me still,
through the gift of art.

Not just for me, but for others to see—
these letters reveal what He's done in me.
Hope for the broken, light in the night,
a better way shines when you step into His light.

Through joy and through pain,
through loss and through gain,
my soul finds release
in only one Name.

So I'll keep on writing as long as I live—
each verse a reflection of all He gives.
Every line pours love,
my devotion increases…
these are my Love Letters to Jesus

FINGERPRINTS

A blank canvas is a work of art;
I take this ink and pour out my heart—
Putting my feelings on display,
Hoping someone reads this
And finds the Lord today.

Every sunset still takes me by surprise—
God loves me enough
To keep opening my eyes.

Time doesn't slow;
there's no time to waste.
So love as many as you can—
Do it with haste.

In the blink of an eye,
It could all end today.
So be careful—
We're remembered by the words we say.

I'm leaving fingerprints on this world,
Trying to make my mark—
A legacy of light
That shines through the dark.

I'll use what God gave me;
I pray others will see—
It's all about Him,
The love that set me free.

Yes, bad decisions come with a price;
My loved ones had to pay,
And that cut like a knife.

But God loved me
When I wasn't even trying.
He saved me
When my soul was dying.

He left the ninety-nine to find me,
Though I was stubborn and blind.
Now I just call it grace—
A love undefined.

Real love—
It won't let others drown.
There's only one place
That kind of love is found.

This is my story;
It's intense—
But His mercy shines bright
Through my fingerprints.

A blank canvas is a work of art;
I take this ink and pour out my heart.
And if one soul is saved
Through the words I say,
Then these fingerprints
Have pointed the way.

WIN SOULS

Win souls—make friends.
Love no matter what—
that's where life begins.

Never underestimate
the power of being kind;
it's in the darkest places
that your light will shine.

You don't need a pulpit
to preach what's true—
just a heart on fire,
and a life bearing fruit.

No matter how they treat you,
wish them peace.
You win the moment
you choose to release.

Let go of the pain,
learn from mistakes.
Speak life—
even when your voice shakes.

Don't just talk about Jesus—
show them the way.
Let your life preach louder
than the words you say.

The harvest is plenty,
but the workers are few.
Be the difference
in all that you do.

Pray for the lost—
even for your foes.
He left the ninety-nine
just to save those.

When life tries to take,
still choose to give.
That's how the faithful
are called to live.

Your crown isn't down here—
so don't be concerned.
You were bought with a price—
now it's your turn.

Don't sweat the small things—
just dance and be free.
Grace already gave you
a new identity.

Someone is watching—
you don't even know.
Your courage might help
their faith to grow.

So don't back down.
Keep standing tall.
Never live to make
someone else feel small.

A soul is worth more
than silver or gold.
So speak life—
even when your heart feels cold.

It's not about fame,
applause, or a stage—
it's about freedom, salvation,
and breaking the cage.

So walk in love,
stand in grace.
The Gospel breathes through
how you run your race.

And when it's done,
and this life rolls by—
may Heaven be full
because you said, "Here am I.

SECTION TWO:

WAR (Fighting the Battles)

RAW EMOTIONS

Raw emotions cut me deep,
Running on empty, climbing the steep.

I tried my best, but still couldn't see—
Every word they spoke kept wounding me.

I carried a weight too heavy to bear;
Shame pressed me down until I gasped for air.
But even there, God whispered my name,
And His mercy covered my guilt and shame.

I built a wall, thinking I had to hide,
But His love broke through and pulled
me outside.
I crawled before I learned to stand,
But now I walk, held in His hands.

I share the truth, though some resist,
But I can't stay silent—God insists.
No need for disguise;
I press ahead with open eyes.

Don't look at me—I'm only dust.
Look to the One in whom I trust.
I've said it before, I'll say it again:
I don't fear people; I lean on Him.

Call me foolish, call me misplaced,
But His Spirit has marked me with grace.

One thing about sheep—they know His voice.
The world may mock, but I've made my choice.
I'm not here to boast; I'm here to show—
It's Christ in me that makes me whole.

THE CALLING IN MY HEART

I can't ignore the calling in my heart—
to return to my first love.
But where do I start?

The struggles I've faced
have taught me to see:
my purpose is to reach lost souls,
because Christ set me free.

No one has to understand
or agree with how I live.
What I carry inside
is what I must give.

A testimony strong enough
to shake the gates of hell wide;
if you need proof,
just ask how I survived.

Anyone who's never been pulled
from the depths of despair
could never understand
like those who have—
that's why they care.

My journey gets muddy at times,
and yes, I fall.
But God never condemns me;
He reminds me that I have what it takes
through it all.

My heart breaks daily
when I see people bound in chains.
That's why I introduce them to Christ—
the One who reigns.

Addiction steals some beautiful souls;
I've seen it far too many times.
So that's why I pour out my heart
and put them into these rhymes.

In hopes that someone will see,
and pray for change.
I promise you this—
you will never be the same.

Nothing hurts more
than feeling like you have no purpose.
People judge by looks,
and not what's beneath the surface.

But I remember those
who showed me kindness
when I felt dead inside.
I'll never forget the ones
who lifted my head
and set aside their pride.

Because the one struggling with addiction
is someone you can see.
And the truth is—
that person could be you or me.

We're all addicted to something,
but judgment drives people away.
So will we choose to love deeply,
or keep turning away?

I've seen too much
to stay silent.
The world's hate is real;
it can turn so violent.

This world needs mercy and grace.
And those who've been broken
know how to embrace.

The time is short—
a vapor, if I'm being honest.
All I'm standing on
is God's promise.

So thankful to be set apart,
I'll live and die
for the calling in my heart.

ME VS. ME

I was born in sin—
the struggle runs deep.
The roads I've taken
still haunt my sleep.

I thought the enemy was people,
but that's not the case.
The enemy was staring
me dead in the face.

Me vs. me—
only God really knows
the battles I fight,
and the scars it shows.

Religious spirits
try to take their stand,
but I evict every lie—
they can't claim this land.

Their whispers and shade
aim straight for my heart,
but they can't shake
what God set apart.

His blood bought me,
and it gave me a voice.
All glory to God—
in Him, I rejoice.

Why can I rejoice?
Because He pulled me out
from the pits of hell—
that's why I praise.
And if people don't like it, oh well.

What can I tell people
from the battles I've survived?
That Jesus is the reason
I'm still alive.

To anyone who feels
like they're too far gone—
it's only a season,
and you're not alone.

Every trial is a lesson,
a test in disguise.
But wisdom looks deeper
than the natural eyes.

Me vs. me—
the struggle is real.
But grace is the anthem
that teaches me to heal.

Victory is certain,
though the war's not through—
because Jesus has already
made all things new.

HIP-HOP RAISED ME,
BUT GOD'S GRACE SAVED ME

Hip-hop raised me,
but God's grace saved me.
I know a thing or two about beats
and how music can make you feel—
but it wasn't until I met Jesus
that I found something real.

Now, I'm far from perfect.
Some days I take two steps forward,
then stumble five steps back.
The devil stays busy,
but I've learned how to fight back.

The cost is high
when you're trying to reach the lost.
I've asked myself more than once,
"Lord, how much does it cost?"

But this is sincere,
and it runs deep in me.
To anyone who thinks
you can't make it out—
yes, you can.
And I pray you see.

I was never the type
to follow the rules.
I never fit in
with the crowd.
I'm part of the few
who made it out,
so I don't stay quiet—
I get real loud.

What does this have to do with hip-hop?
Let me explain:
the music is smooth,
but it can leave you crying in the rain.

The world's view of hip-hop
was everything to me.
It carried me away,
but it never set me free.

I loved Tupac, Eminem,
and Mary J. Blige—
songs that held my pain,
and soothed my cries.
On bad days, I'd hit play
and drift far from home,
until the beat wore off
and turned my heart to stone.

Hip-hop gave me a rush,
and I can't lie—
I had a crush.

But then God started speaking to my soul.
He told me plain:
"Daughter, let those demons go."

People will say,
"There's nothing wrong with hip-hop…"
and I used to agree—
until I realized
how much it truly hurt me.

'Cause God spoke to my soul,
and He opened my eyes:
that music carries spirits,
and demons hide in disguise.

Now that I walk with Jesus,
the sound has changed.
I hear chains in the rhythm,
and poison in the veins.

This world revolves around music—
and this is a war.
So I guard my heart
like never before.

Hip-hop raised me,
but grace rewrote my name.
What I found in Jesus
will never be the same.

Beats can move your body,
but only Christ can save your soul.
Now my song is different—
He's the one in control.

SOUL WHAT

When it comes to certain matters,
I don't play around.
The only reason I'm standing here today
is because I've been found.

Not by anything I've done—
let me make that clear.
It's only by the grace of God
that I'm still here.

Some people might shrug and say, "So what?"
But I flip it different: "Soul What."
That's S-O-U-L, W-H-A-T—
the story of a soul set free.

So what if I was broken?
Soul What—now I'm whole.
So what if I was empty?
Soul What—He saved my soul.

In the midnight hour,
I was broken and alone,
chained by fear,
with a heart made of stone.

There was a longing no man could fill,
a wound so deep
only His hand could heal.

He caught my tears,
pulled me from the night.
Now I walk as a soldier—
not by strength, but by His might.

There is beauty in the struggle,
even when my eyes can't see.
Still I lift my hands in praise
for all He's done for me.

So when they say, "So what?"
I answer with my life:
let me tell you about my Jesus,
the One who brought me back to life.

And if they ask again, "So what?"
I'll smile and boldly say:
Soul What—it's all about Jesus.
And that's why I live this way.

ALMOST AIN'T HOLY

Almost ain't holy.
It tried to fold me,
but the grip slipped,
and the good Lord told me:
"Let it go."

All the pain?
It serves a greater cause.
One thing about me—
I'll never hide my flaws.

Where do wildflowers grow?
In the dirt—
that's how you know.

We came from dust,
and to dust, we will return.
Almost ain't holy…
so watch it burn.

This battle's been long,
but victory is my song.
There's a war cry in my spirit—
it's been there all along.

Even if no one goes with me,
still, I will follow.
Without purpose,
life is empty and hollow.

If we don't practice what we preach,
then we've got nothing to teach.
People are searching for something real.
People are broken,
and they need to heal.

I've been through a lot—
can't deny that, it's true.
But these wings are emerging…
and I'm about to break through.

The light of dawn is on the brink,
so I take my tears
and mix them with ink.

I have to stay humble,
there's no room for pride.
The power and the kingdom
are His to provide.

Almost ain't holy—
a halfway walk won't do.
Take me where You need me, Lord—
make me brand new.

I know I'll reap
exactly what I sow.
So plant me in Your presence,
and tell me where to go.

Almost ain't holy—
I refuse to stay bound.
Pour out the Holy Ghost,
'til Your glory surrounds.

LET IT BURN

I've traveled down some hard roads,
Got lost somewhere in between—
The girl who used to be real sweet
She turned out pretty mean.

I spent years in my addiction,
I mistreated all my friends.
And when I look back on my life,
I hate the way sin wins.

But Someone kept pulling me close—
Oh, how I love that Holy Ghost.
A spark was hidden deep in me,
A flame the darkness couldn't seize.

I can't go back and fix the past—
That girl I used to be.
But I can point you to the Man
Who came and set me free.

Your Spirit never let me go,
A whisper turned into a glow.
That fire rose against the night,
And filled my soul with holy light.

When I was low,
Your grace lifted me up.
You broke my chains,
And You filled my cup.

I won't make excuses
For how hard life has been for me.
I'll lift the name of Jesus,
Who died and rose to set me free.

So let it burn, let it blaze—
My life redeemed, my hands are raised.
The battle is over, Jesus has won.
My life isn't over—
It's only just begun.

LAY DOWN MY STONE

How we see someone
can change the flow.
It says more about our character
than the stones we throw.

Does the Bible not tell us?
We reap what we sow.

An eye for an eye—
do the math:
mercy outweighs wrath.

We all see others through broken eyes,
Quick to assume, too slow to realize.
Our vision's clouded by pride and pain,
Pointing the finger, and forgetting our stain.

I've held that stone, it weighed me down,
My proof I was right, my claim to the crown.
But God leaned close and whispered a psalm:
"Lay it down, child—be still, be calm."

So I hit my knees
and said, "Lord, You're right.
I realize now—
it's never been my fight."

When all is said,
and all is shown,
I will humble myself...
and lay down my stone.

SEND ME, I'LL GO

In my rebellion, I was relentless—
yet You never left my side.
Like Jonah in the belly of the whale,
I was swallowed by pride.

Afraid to step on toes?
That won't win souls for the Kingdom
and the crown.
But thank God, You stepped in
and turned my life around.

Nineveh needs to know.
So send me, Lord—I'll go.

No more running,
just moving in the right direction.
Even in my darkest hour,
I could feel Your protection.

I see no enemies,
though I know they're lurking near.
But because of how far You've brought me,
I can love them—
and cast out fear.

I'm different now,
a new creation in Christ.
No more silence—
just a love that's fire, not ice.

What they think
doesn't change my pace.
The mission is set,
and I'm running this race.

There's a fourth Man in the fire,
and I will not bow to man.
My eyes are on the Savior,
and my faith is in His plan.

The harvest is ready,
the world must know.
Send me, Lord—
I'll go.

A REBEL IN REVERSE

A rebel in reverse,
with a heart rearranged.
He rolled the stone away—
and I've been forever changed.

I don't hold grudges
against those who talk behind my back.
I pray for them,
and I give the enemy no ground to attack.

I see no enemies,
only souls that need to be seen—
the way He sees me,
forgiven, redeemed, and walking free.

If you're scared to be different,
you'll fade into the crowd.
But my praise is a weapon—
that's why I'm soul loud.

There's no dialing it down,
so don't tell me how to praise.
I love this deeply,
'cause I remember the hell I used to raise.

To whom much is given,
much will be required.
I owe my life to the cross—
and my spirit stays on fire.

He rolled the stone away,
so I can't go back to a hardened heart.
When people see me,
I want them to notice—I've been set apart.

No chains can bind me,
no grave can claim.
The rebel in me
now burns with His flame.

Souls are at stake—
and this means war.
I can't go back
to the way I was before.

Now every thought
leads me straight to one thing:
How can I bring others closer
to Jesus—the King?

A rebel in reverse,
with a heart rearranged.
He rolled the stone away—
and I'll never be the same.

WARFARE WINGS

I chose the butterfly
to mark this fight—
a bloodline drawn in chalk,
but grace rewrote my life.

Searching for purpose
on battleground fields,
I fell on my face,
drowning in the pills.

I bowed to my idols—
it's sad, but true.
Lost in the darkness,
I didn't know what to do.

But the wings…
they shimmer through pain—
not fragile ornaments,
but proof I remain.

They rise from the ashes,
they spread through the night,
they carry my story,
they testify of His light.

Illuminating my back,
I rise with grace.
What once felt like weakness
now finds its place.

From ashes to altitude,
I survived the fall.
These wings are not for show—
they're weapons, after all.

They're warfare wings,
the reason my soul sings.
Every step I take,
I don't walk alone—
I'm reaching for Heaven,

for it is my home.

Forged in fire,
through battles I've overcome,
I'll keep flying forward,
'til the war is won.

And when I land
before His throne,
these warfare wings
will lead me home.

EYES ON JESUS

Without vision, we perish.
Without integrity, too—
A dream without Christ
will never come true.

We need the Body of Christ—
every gift, every voice, every call.
There is no "I" in team,
and divided, we all fall.

Our focus should be on God alone,
yet too often we point fingers
with a judgmental tone.

We've been warned against division—
so how can we claim the truth
and still walk in indecision?

If we're not reaching for souls,
then what are we trying to achieve?
Are we leaning on our own strength,
or on the One we say we believe?

It's not about black, white, yellow, or red—
it's about the blood
that raised us from the dead.

So why do we magnify flaws,
and act like we're the judge?
Why do we monitor steps,
instead of lifting with love?

Jesus didn't die for us to compare,
He died so the lost would know He's there.

There's a harvest waiting,
and the workers are few.
The question remains—
Will He send me? Will He send you?

So let's set aside gossip,
competition, and pride.
Let's lay down our titles
and fight side by side.

We are one body—
many parts, one King.
And when we move together,
hell begins to shake and scream.

So lift your eyes to Jesus—
He is the goal,
the reason we run,
the anchor for our souls.

And if the world is watching,
let them see what's true:
the love of Christ alive
in me and in you.

WAR ROOM CRY

In the war room, I cry,
staring through the skies.
Deception speaks,
but the devil lies.

I strap on truth
until my helmet fits tight.
I draw my sword—
I'm built for the fight.

I call on Jesus,
He is my solid rock.
No need for crowds,
I stand with the flock.

With gospel shoes, I walk in peace,
and even when storms refuse to cease,
He rewrote my story,
I'll never be the same—
to God be the glory,
forever His name.

The war cries loud,
and the thunder rolls,
but I press on
with eternal goals.

A love so fierce,
He wore thorns for a crown.
The blood ran deep,
and the veil came down.

The devil tried to drown me,
but grace pulled me through.
Now angels surround me,
and my song is new.

My past was messy,
ugly and raw—
but look at my Savior,
I stand in awe.

There's beauty now
in what I've been through,
so I'll keep writing
'til my mission's through.

Tell the world—
it's all about You.

SECTION THREE:

BLOODLINE
(Legacy & Redemption)

GOD, GROWTH, AND GOALS

There's something about growth—
it stretches you,
breaks you,
and sometimes tears you apart…
but the goal
is to shape you
into a masterpiece of God's heart.

The crushing and the pressing
cut deep in my chest.
I don't always like it,
but I still trust—
God knows best.

No greater love
than the One who laid it all down.
This battle is real,
and I'm running for my crown.

One way or another,
His promise will unfold.
He carried me through
when I thought I'd fold.

The enemy deceives,
setting traps for the kill…
but I'm not afraid to die—
let's be real.

For to die is to live;
it's hard to comprehend.
But every scar
and every trial
serves His plan
in the end.

God is shaping my soul
to look like His own.
And even in the hurt,
I know I'm not alone.

And when it's finished,
don't clap for me—
clap for the King
who wrote my story.

I'll boast in my weakness,
He gets the glory.
Even when the cuts run deep,
they serve His purpose.
My identity is in Christ,
so I'm never worthless.

Face to the dirt,
and bruises that burn…
but even in hurt,
I'll praise Him while I learn.

This calling of mine?
To help save souls.
That's the heartbeat:
God, Growth, and Goals.

Not chasing the world,
but the crown He's set.
I'll run this race—
and I'll have no regret.

TO MY KIDS (A.K.A. MY TEAM)

To my kids—or should I say my crew,
Y'all are calm, cool, and handsome too.
You've been my rock through highs and lows,
Laid-back legends—everybody knows.

You spoiled me rotten, lifted me high,
Always encouraging—never asking why.
Even when life tried to knock me down,
You stood beside me, never wore a frown.

You're sweet, you're funny, you crack me UP,
Your charm keeps overflowin' my cup.
But every time I post a throwback look…
It's, "MAMA! Please—not on the Book!"

LOL—I don't listen, though.
I'm like, "BRO…"
Then I hit post and play it off slow.

IYKYK, you just roll your eyes,
But still you love me—and that's the prize.
From silly jokes to the tightest bond,
We laugh, we pray, we roll as one.

Forever your mama, through thick and thin—
Proud of my sons, my heart, my kin.

STILL, IT WAS LOVE

It was love—
that carried me through.
Not my strength, not my will,
but the One who makes all things new.

When times get tight,
it is the Word that brings light.
I can't explain it…
but if I could, it might
sound like this—

a love so rare, I can hardly resist.

This isn't Romeo and Juliet—
no poison at the end, no regret.

It's a love that lasts for eternity,
calling me deeper in.
I've come to learn it's less about things
and more about faithful friends.

All those nights I thought I was alone,
Heaven kept whispering,
"Daughter, come home."

I chased the highs—
it all led to vanity.
The lows nearly broke
my sanity.

But still it was love
that kept on calling.
He caught me in mercy
and stopped me from falling.

I can write all these poems,
turn them into books,
and still get lost
in how it looks.

I can't take any of it with me—
Ecclesiastes made it clear:
all is empty
without love and family near.

It was love—
not empty things—
that lifted me up
and gave me wings.

Written in His blood,
the story is true:
the grave lost its power,
and love brought me to You.

TAKE ME DOWN TO THE RIVER

Take me down to the river,
as I shake, tremble, and shiver.
I'm in desperate need of a risen Savior—
Lord, baptize me in the Jordan of Your favor.

Wash away my sins,
make me white as snow.
Dip me seven times—
please, don't let me go.

I'm too muddy, and I need
to be cleansed.
But when I look around,
all I see are my sins.

I've been washed up,
so I know how it goes.
I can't find my friends
when surrounded by foes.

I've felt the sting
as thcy turned me away—
but even in rejection,
You drew me to stay.

I try to guide the lost
to the One who is true—
but they push You away,
just like I used to do.

Then again, I didn't want You either.
But look at me now—
You turned Saul into Paul,
and all I can say is, WOW.

How long will I run this race?
Until the finish,
until the crown,
until I see Jesus,
and lay it all down.

THE POTTER AND THE CLAY

A masterpiece is created;
the Potter and the clay are intimately related.

You shape the mold—
in Your hands, You alone hold.

All the pieces, You know them well.
You take Your time—inhale, exhale.

Let it breathe as You work,
to mold me into something new.
Your hands are upon me, God—
Your craftsmanship is true.

Nothing is wasted, nothing rushed;
You're still good when my soul feels crushed.

Even when a piece of me shatters,
and I don't want anyone else to see,
I still thank You, God,
for never giving up on me.

A Father's love has no end;
it's poured out without measure.
You transform worn-out clay
into beautiful treasure.

I love the Potter, and He loves me.
And even though I'm not perfect,
that's what I want the world to see.

A masterpiece takes time—
and beautiful things
are born from heartache and pain.

Because as clay, in order to thrive,
we need the rain.

Even through the fire,
You make me strong.
What felt like breaking
was shaping all along.

A masterpiece is created;
the Potter and the clay are intimately related.

I love Him more than words can say—
He is the Potter,
and I am the clay.

I CAN ONLY IMAGINE

I can only imagine,
as her stones hit the sand.
She must have looked up at Him in shame,
as He reached down for her hand.

To be honest,
I picture myself there too—
trying to find the courage
to look into His eyes,
if only I could take off my disguise.

How someone like Jesus could love me
is beyond anything I could ever dream of,
even if I tried.
And I've come to realize—

Like her, I've stumbled;
most of my problems are tied to pride.
But grace still found me,
even when I tried to hide.

I've been afraid that if I'm honest,
He'll leave me high and dry.
How could anyone possibly understand
the tears I cry?

"Let him who is without sin
cast the first stone."
I wonder what He wrote in the sand
that made them leave her alone.

He didn't just speak—
He became the Light.
What words did He whisper
that shattered the night?

I can only imagine,
as her stones hit the sand.
She must have looked up at Him in shame,
as He reached down for her hand.

TOUGH AS NAILS

Tough as nails—
the hands that bore the scars of the cross,
wounds that bled freedom for the lost.

A debt I could never repay,
even if I tried.
I weep as I reflect
on all the weight He bore inside.

Jesus endured lashes, mockery, and shame,
as they spat in His face and cursed His name.
Who else would take our place?
Only love could bear that kind of grace.

He came for the black sheep—
and if not for Him, I'd be six feet deep.
But love like this—John 3:16—
breaks every chain and wipes every slate clean.

Nothing in this world can stand in the way;
Jesus is the reason I'm standing today.

I've been released from a prison unseen—
now I walk by faith,
with a mind that's clean.

His mercy prevails.
That's what it means to be
tough as nails.

But that grave couldn't hold Him—He rose in
power,
defeated death in His final hour.
Now I live because He lives—forever free,
blood-bought, unshaken, and walking in victory.

SOLD OUT

As a child, I spoke like a child,
and even now, I stumble at times.
Words slip out that never should,
then circle heavy in my mind.
I repent, Lord, when I act in haste—
teach me to respond with mercy and grace.

I don't always get it right,
but I'm growing through each test.
When I follow Your Word,
my soul finds joy, and I can rest.

Transformation cuts deep—
it leaves me feeling exposed,
completely stripped and searching
for what only grace bestows.

My knees are worn
from kneeling on the floor,
but that's the posture of battle—
we're soldiers in a war.

Apart from Christ,
I have no reason to live.
But in Your presence,
I see all You freely give.

So I surrender,
laying down my pride.
Every breath and every step
is my choice to decide.

What You've done in my life,
no one else could do.
Yes—I am sold out.
I'm completely sold out to You.

A living sacrifice,
my worship is my vow.
Take all that I am—
I am Yours, here and now.

Sealed by the Lamb,
redeemed, set free.
I'm sold out forever,
because Your blood runs in me

INHERITANCE

This inheritance comes at a cost—
I'm reaching out for the weary and lost.
I've laid my life down for this cause,
and believe me, I don't need your handclaps
or applause.

Because when you've seen what I've seen,
you can't claim you don't know.
This mission means everything,
and I refuse to let it go.

I was just like that wayward son—
I squandered everything I had.
And when I think of the time I wasted,
it still makes me sad.

So hear me now—

Don't test the same flames I had to walk through;
the scars still choke.
Don't gamble with your soul
or treat life like a joke.
Don't push the edge thinking God will see
you through,
because sin will consume everything—
and still come back for you.

Not every wound heals clean;
some bleed in places never seen.
Some nights you'll still taste the dirt
from where sin dragged you in to flirt.

I can't go back in time,
and I'll never turn back again—
unless it's only to testify
about how much I hate sin.

And understand this—
this inheritance isn't silver or gold.
It's not land, or stocks, or keys you can hold.

It's an eternal inheritance,
paid in full, signed in love…
a gift from our Father,
who reigns from above.

POWER IN THE BLOOD

There is power in the blood—ask me why.
Without that sacrifice, my soul would run dry.
He didn't come for the water; He came for
the sinner.
The blood ran down, and it flowed to my inner.

I strive for more—
I can't stand to be less.
Why settle for crumbs
when I can have God's best?

He's shown me too much—
I had to push past the crowd.
This was my war cry,
and I cried out loud.

"Who touched me?" He asked as He passed by.
"It's me, Lord—please hear my cry!"
Pressing through the crowd, shame in my eyes,
my insecurities screamed, and my soul agonized.

Ashamed of my past,
my head to the ground—
where in the world
could hope be found?

But He didn't shame me
or turn me away.
He lifted my head,
and He chose to stay.

I was the woman at the well,
trying to fill what only God could fill.
Too ashamed for Him to know
all the men I ran to,
and the secrets I couldn't kill.

I numbed the pain with pills and highs,
held captive to the lies.
A terrible mom in my own eyes,
even though my babies

still looked at me with love in their cries.

I was dying in silence,
but He met me mid-shame—
not with a lecture,
but with mercy,
and He called me by name.

The bleeding stopped—
but more than that:
peace took root,
and now I bear fruit.

There is power in the blood—ask me why.
Without that sacrifice, my life would run dry.
So if you're broken and bound by shame,
call on the blood—
it breaks every chain.

GRACE WALK

The more I walk this narrow way,
the more I've learned to still my tongue—
starving the serpent's lies each day,
refusing the songs he's sung.

The more I whisper "I,"
the more pride tries to reign.
But heaven answers softly,
"Child, lean on My name."

Each morning rises
with mercy's embrace.
And more than anything,
I seek Your face.

Grace is given to me,
so I give it away—
the treasures worth keeping
are love, and loyalty's stay.

This race is not easy;
the path is not light.
But faith is my lantern,
still burning at night.

Thank You, Jesus,
for the breath that I take.
Though some days I falter,
and tremble, and shake.

Yet somehow, Lord,
You draw truth out of me,
revealing a faith
I never thought I would see.

I'm humbled, Lord,
to behold You one day,
to lift endless thanks
for this gift of grace.

A holy revelation—
You speak to my soul,
even when silence
becomes my control.

Your blood carved this pathway,
Your love keeps the stride.
And each step I take in grace
is walking with You by my side.

I NEED A FRIEND

Love is a river that overflows.
Love is a seed that forever grows.
Love is the courage that steps right in.
Love is the blood that removes my sin.
Lord, it's me again—
and I need a friend.

I've tried things my way,
but they never work out.
And when I feel like I've failed You,
the enemy floods my mind with doubt.

Life is one long test—
but onward, Christian soldier,
I will give my best.

I have my battles, and sometimes I fear
that people will see through and judge me here.
But truth be told, it's not their view—
what truly matters is what You see in me… and
what I see in You.

The only thing that matters
is that Your will be done.
When I walk through the valleys,
You shine like the sun.

I don't seek the praise
that belongs to You.
Your truth alone
will carry me through.

I love how You love me—
no act, no show.
And I'll only go
where You tell me to go.

Without You, I'm nothing—
my life wouldn't matter to me.
But You are everything
I was always meant to be.

Love is a river that overflows.
Love is the courage that always knows—
even in the fall,
You will still call.
Love is the blood
that covers it all.

Lord, it's me again…
and I still need a friend.
But I trust the One
who's with me from beginning to end.

DEAR GOD

Help me not to become bitter,
but to call on You—
for Your love is so sweet.
This is the cry of my heart
as I sit at Your feet.

If You would take this pain away,
I could finally breathe.
Here's my heart—
it's heavy on my sleeve.

Just one touch is all it takes.
My mind is weary, and it aches.
There are no words left—
I've said them all.
I've shed so many tears,
and I know You've seen them fall.

I can endure a lot,
but this feels like more than I can take.
How much more must I bear
before I break?

Everything in me is being tested…
yet here I am—still invested.

And if one more person
tries to crush my spirit—
Lord, come on…
I know You hear it.

Please help me—
or at least help my unbelief.
I'm drowning in this ocean of grief.

I find rest in You,
but I'm tired all the time.
Watching my loved ones suffer
doesn't feel fine.

Everyone keeps saying, "It's okay,"—
but it's not how I feel.
I'm done pretending…
Lord, I need something real.

I just hope You hear my cries,
because life gets tough—
especially when the devil
whispers his lies.

I've come too far
to let people drag me down.
Only in You
is true hope found.

Nothing worth having is easy, I suppose—
but here I am,
still standing on all ten toes.

Jesus…

Help me not to grow bitter,
but to keep calling on You.
Your love is my anchor,
faithful and true.

This is the cry of my heart
as I sit at Your feet—
and even in the storm,
Your grace is complete.

PROMISES

I never promised the road would be easy,
and I never said you wouldn't fall.
But I did promise to love you—
through every misstep, through it all.

I never said the answers would come
as quickly as you'd hope they might,
but I did promise to walk beside you,
holding your hand through every night.

I never promised you'd be spared
from heartache or from pain,
but I did promise we'd dance together
in the middle of the rain.
And every tear you've ever cried
will never be in vain.

I never said you'd always get it right,
or that life would always feel good—
but I did promise to be right there
when you're misunderstood.

I never said you wouldn't feel
belittled, lost, or small,
but I did promise the world would see
that in Me, you stand tall.

I never promised every day
would be free from sorrow or despair,
but I did promise that joy would come—
and hope would still be there.

I never make a promise
I don't intend to keep.
My Word is faithful;
My love runs deep.

I cannot lie – what I've spoken is true,
Every promise I've made, I'll keep for you.

THIS IS MY TESTIMONY

He brought the light back into my eyes without
condemnation or any of the lies
What you see here is beauty for ashes, and still
I rise

Binded, I was tied up and blinded buried in my
past, I couldn't move on. Welcome to the story of
my life always looking for a place when I
already belong.

Emotions, well dare I say that they took my
thoughts and ran them deep into the oceans.
Soon enough the waves, they came crashing in,
and there I lay all washed up naked on the shore
in all of my sin.

Now going back and forth. It's the same as
getting nowhere fast, and if I could sum up my
life in only three words, they would be in a flash.

All my life I had to fight, but it was never flesh
and blood. It was me throwing my pearls to the
swine while we wrestled in the mud.

Now I said that I would kill him dead if he ever
lays his hands on me again, I've had my
encounters with Harpo, and life it's no fairytale,
my friend

Each day that I have, I'm blessed to be alive
considering where I've been. I'm grateful that I
even survived.

For the people who want to know and understand
my story, I'll put it like this to God, be the glory

In all honesty, all I remember are bits and pieces
truth is the drugs, Fried, my brain, and traded out
my smarts for feces.

My days grew dark and my heart was ripped from my chest. I wish that I could say to you that I tried my best, but I'd be lying. The fact is that I allowed the enemy to stab and jab at me repeatedly as I lay there dying.

The chaos screeched like nails on a chalkboard, and the sound nearly drove me out of my mind. I was looking for a way out, but that road became harder and harder to find.

I hurt a lot of people and I didn't care I thought to myself, why should I after all life sure did hand me my fair share.

I cried out most days without crying at all the bombs inside my head exploded, and I built walls. I hid myself behind the shame, and I made them that hurt me the place to blame.

I would put up a guard so that I couldn't feel and the game plan was to take just enough to help me deal. But it only led me deeper in.

I was hanging on by a thread, and the thin of my skin. For the life of me I couldn't get a head I mean, how was I supposed to? I literally could've been in the cast of The Walking Dead.

Looking back now I see how everyone tried their best to tell me. Man addiction is scary and all it ever did was fail me.

Someone help me please I prayed in a panic. My life had shattered right before my very eyes, and suddenly I was frantic.

Tell me, where do you turn when all your bridges are burned. It's time to face the music and you're the one who never learns.

This is more than a wake-up call. It's the moment you realize that you have been searching for something with no purpose at all.

As for me, I was the boy who cried wolf one time too many. I was incredibly loved by my family and friends, still am but didn't appreciate them any.

I was the woman at the well. I blew every dime
that I had, and was headed straight for hell

I thought that I was too messed up and damaged
beyond repair so with razor Sharp rebellion, I let
Delilah in on the secret to my strength, and she
gladly took my hair

I grew faint, and to tell you that I am proud of
myself or where I've been well, I ain't

But then a voice began calling me in. I've heard
it before, but then I heard it again. A gentle one
this time, soft and full of grace.

And as sure, as the Sun shines he reached down
and inside of me he slowly begin to take the
taste, and I tell you right now there is not a man
alive who can take his place.

He catches my tears. You see the opinion, of man
and what he thinks of me has weighed me down
for years. And you wouldn't know this, but me
doing this spoken word in front of all you guys,
is also my facing one of my biggest fears.

But here I stand, and I have to say that God is good and life is grand. How amazing to know that it's all part of his plan

Then God said, let there be light surely he was thinking of both you and me. I believe it was that very moment that he set the captives free.

And as bad as I was, he never did see me that way. Standing here redeemed and bought with the blood he sees only his son Jesus Christ today

Though I'm not perfect and prone to make mistakes. I'm worthy, so I'll carry my cross no matter the stakes. I'll do whatever it takes.

Freedom is a choice and it's up to us whether or not we use it as a voice. If no one knows your story, they will never understand your praise

Set your goals. Make your Mark and do it with a blaze. And SOUL-WHAT if no one likes it and by the way.

That's "S O U L-W H A T" and it all boils down
to this. That this is my soul and I'm the only one
who's gonna answer for me

So, without condemnation or any of the lies, my
prayer here is that he will bring the light back
into someone else's eyes

This is my testimony,
Beauty for ashes and still I rise.

MIRACLE MATH

Five thousand people,
divided in plan,
sitting in sections—
God's glory was grand.

Five loaves. Two fish.
Twelve disciples raised their brows:
"Send them away—what do we do now?
We don't have the food,
and we've got no money to spend."
But oh, how our God
shows up like a friend.

He said, "Watch Me work.
Just place it in My hands."
And what wasn't enough
became more than they planned.

Now do the math—
five thousand, not a small crowd.
They sat down in groups—
and the silence grew loud.

But wait—it wasn't just the men.
There were women and children too.
Look at God—
He really came through.

That's Kingdom math,
miraculous and intense.
When you give it to Jesus,
it starts to make sense.

He multiplies fully—
not halfway, not just some—
but enough to remind us
where blessings come from.

He broke it. He blessed it.
Then fed every face.
What looked like a little
became a feast of grace.

It makes you wonder,
makes you pause and think—
His miracles multiply,
like truth written in ink.

So why do I worry?
Why do I stress?
With God, I'm provided for—
He knows what is best.

So I sit back
and trust Him with my biz,
'cause the little in my hands
gets multiplied in His.

BUTTERFLY BLOODLINE

I was broken—
shattered wings,
a soul addicted,
chained to empty things.

The devil whispered, "You'll never fly—
your story ends here."
But God reached down,
and pulled me near.

From ashes, He raised me—
His mercy rewrote my name.
Every scar became a testimony,
every wound a flame.

I've crawled through darkness,
but He gave me light.
I've lost my strength,
but He taught me to fight.

Butterflies are fragile—
that's what they say.
But these wings were forged
in war, in clay.
They shimmer with grace,
they're marked with scars.
Each beat declares,
"I know whose I are."

This bloodline isn't curses,
it's not chains, it's not shame.
It's redemption flowing deeper—
sealed in Jesus' name.

I was the woman at the well,
the one reaching through the crowd,
the sinner caught in silence,
but His mercy spoke loud.

He said, "Daughter, you're free—
go and sin no more."
And the rebel in reverse
walked out of that war.

Now I'm sold out,
my soul set aflame.
I walk in His promises,
unashamed of His name.

This is my inheritance,
this is my song.
Not who I was—
but who I've become all along.

From blood to wings,
from cross to crown,
what the enemy built
was all torn down.

So hear me clear—
this life is divine.
I'm a child of the King—
of the Butterfly Bloodline.

ACKNOWLEDGEMENTS

First and foremost, I want to thank my Lord and Savior, Jesus Christ, for saving my life. Every page of this book is a reflection of His mercy and grace. Without Him, I wouldn't be here.

To my family and my kids—you are my heart. You stood by me through every storm, loved me at my lowest, and reminded me of who I was when I had forgotten. Your faith in me has been one of God's greatest gifts, and I carry that love everywhere I go.

To the kindest people—the ones who treated me with love and compassion regardless of how I felt—thank you. Your steady kindness was a reminder of the Father's heart, and it carried me when I couldn't carry myself.

I'm grateful for the discipleship programs that poured into me: Bethel Colony of Mercy and Vessels of Mercy. You taught me discipline, structure, and unconditional love. You believed in me when I didn't believe in myself, and I'll never forget the seeds you planted in my life.

To my friends, near and far, and to the Body of Christ—thank you for your prayers and encouragement. They didn't just lift me up once; they still lift me up today. Every message, every prayer, every word spoken in love has left an imprint on my soul, and I carry that with me.

And finally, to every person battling addiction: you are seen, you are loved, and you are not forgotten. It is an honor to use the gift God has given me to reach souls like yours. This book is my prayer for unity, healing, and hope. May you always know there is power in His blood, and there is freedom in His name.

AUTHOR'S CORNER

Niki Hutchins is a small-town girl from Rutherford County, North Carolina. Growing up, she faced both love and hardship, navigating family struggles and personal battles that shaped her journey. Despite the heartache in her life, God has remained faithful, bringing healing.

Niki has always had a passion for creativity, expressing herself through writing, spoken word, music, acting, dancing, and comedy. She views every gift God has given her as an opportunity to encourage others with honesty and hope.

Delivered from addiction, Niki has been free from drugs for over three years—something she once thought she would never achieve, even for a single day. Her story is living proof that God's grace is stronger than shame or bondage.

She currently resides in Spindale, North Carolina, and cherishes her friends, her family, and nearly everyone she meets. Above all, Niki walks closely with Jesus Christ, her Savior and her best friend, and she looks forward to wherever He leads her in the future—confident that her journey shows no matter where you've been, God can rewrite your future.

Made in the USA
Middletown, DE
23 November 2025